They lived like this in
ANCIENT AFRICA

Author: MARIE NEURATH

Artist: EVELYN WORBOYS

of the Isotype Institute

FRANKLIN WATTS, INC.,
845 Third Avenue, New York 10022

© 1967 Isotype Institute Limited
Published by Franklin Watts, Inc., 845 Third Avenue, New York 10022, U.S.A.
Printed in Great Britain by Purnell & Sons, Ltd

Library of Congress Catalog No. 67—17659

ANCIENT AFRICA

Africa used to be called the dark continent because so little was known about its interior. The early peoples of Egypt, Crete, Greece and Rome knew only the Nile valley and the Mediterranean coast, south of which lay the great Sahara desert, a barrier which they could not cross. Long before the time of these ancient peoples, however, the Sahara was a fertile land where animals and men lived. There are cave paintings of early hunters in places that are now bare rock and sand.

This picture of an elephant, cut into the rock face, is perhaps the oldest of all. Other cave pictures were made generations later.

This man is carrying his bow and arrow.
A tame dog goes hunting with him.
Dogs were among men's earliest companions.

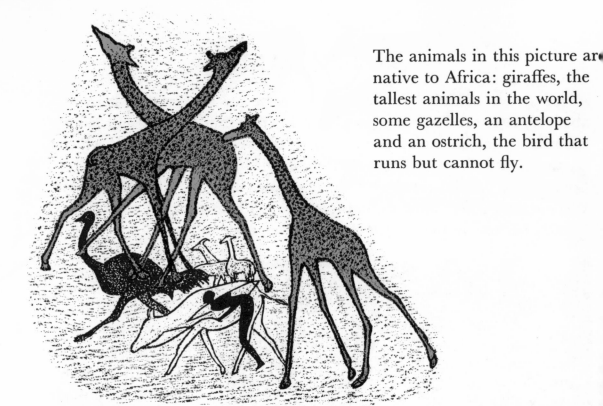

The animals in this picture are native to Africa: giraffes, the tallest animals in the world, some gazelles, an antelope and an ostrich, the bird that runs but cannot fly.

Here we see bowmen running and fighting. One is brandishing a weapon which looks like a throwing stick.

These people were herdsmen. They came after the early hunters.
A dead animal, lying on its back, is being cut up for food.

The man sitting behind the
cow seems to be milking.
Mothers with children are
nearby. Pictures like these
are the oldest documents
of life in Africa.

We are not sure where the people went when they left
the caves. Some may have gone north into Spain, where
similar cave paintings are found. Others may have
moved south, towards the west coast.

5

In tropical Africa the heavy rainfall creates great rivers and forests. The moisture causes so much decay that little remains of early times. But it is less wet in the grasslands that lie between the forests and the desert. Here models of human heads have bee found. They are 2000 years old, and the features are more African than those in the cave paintings. Almost nothing is known about the people wh made them. Later tribes cast heads in brass and bronze, but these are made of clay. We know more about the African tribes of recent times.

They used clay to make pots. These have been burnt black and polished.

Their houses, too, were often built of clay. Some tribes decorated them with moulded pictures or designs. This panel shows a typical African tree, a palm tree. Palm oil was an important food in some parts.

Every tribe grew crops.

Agriculture may have spread from ancient Egypt, but there were not many African plants suitable for cultivation. In later times bananas, yams, maize and cassava were introduced from other lands.

Animals were more plentiful. These figures of a scorpion, a frog, a mudfish and an antelope were carved on an ivory jug.

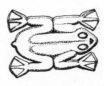

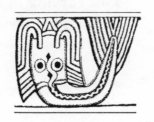

There were fish in the lakes and rivers and along the sea coast.
This picture shows men harpooning fish from boats.
Sometimes special baskets were used. Women waded into shallow water
and plunged them down over a shoal of fish. They took the catch out
through a hole in the top of the basket.

This carving of a fish decorated
the wooden door of a chief's house.

This carving was made for the prow of a canoe by tribesmen near the coast, who lived by fishing and trading. Where the great rivers enter the sea they create muddy swamps in which mangroves grow and boats are the only possible means of transport.

This crocodile decorates a bowl made from a calabash. After the inside of the fruit was removed, the shell could be used as a bowl or a bottle. Spoons were made by cutting a bottle-shaped shell in half lengthwise.

The Bushmen, whose ancestors painted this picture on a cave wall, still live by hunting and gathering wild fruits. Here we see them with their bows. The arrows, tipped with deadly poison, were carried in their headbands.

The more advanced African tribes hunted with iron-tipped spears. They also farmed with tools made of iron; its use may have spread from ancient Egypt 2000 years ago. Many also kept herds of cattle. Here they have made textile designs with animal figures.

Several West African tribes
worked in bronze.
This figure shows a hunter
with his bow, carrying the
antelope he has killed slung
over his shoulders.

This bronze panel shows a
jungle scene. The men, who
are hunting leopards, wear
the same kind of headdress
as the hunter above.

Some tribes lived in towns, and the men and women walked to their fields to work. But in many cases the tribe consisted of small family homesteads scattered amongst the farmlands.

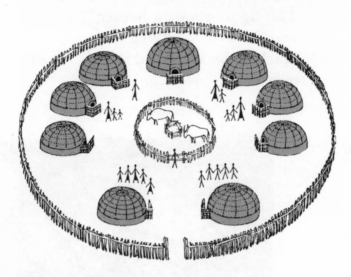

A man might have several wives. Each wife had a hut for herself and her young children. There were special huts for the grown boys and girls.

Each tribe built its huts in a special style. Some were made of wooden frames covered with long grass. Some were of clay with circular walls and cone-shaped roofs. Others were square. The roof might project to form a verandah.

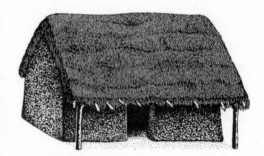

leeping mats were the
ain hut furniture.
hey were woven from
rass. Here are some
eaving patterns. They
re called "the cow's
ye", "the snake" and
the fish".

There might be beds made of bamboo, or else part of the floor of hard
eaten earth was raised to make a bed near the wall. If there were not
nough beds for all the members of the family, their mats were
ut on the floor. Some tribes used neckrests for sleeping.
The neckrests of important people were often elaborately carved.

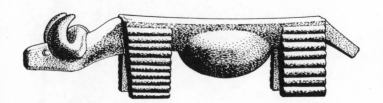

Animals were not widely used for carrying loads, and there were no carts or wheels. People, especially the women, did most of the carrying

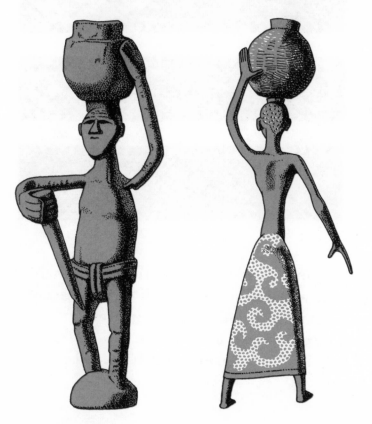

They could balance heavy loads on their heads even while moving about and bending.

The women worked the fields and prepared the food. They used wooden mortars to pound grain or yams.

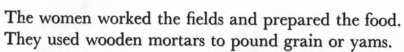

Her young children accompanied a
mother while she worked. The baby
would sleep, tied comfortably to
her back.
When he woke and cried, no matter
where, his mother would stop to
feed him.

Women carried water from the streams, goods
to and from the markets, and produce from
the fields, walking in single file along
the footpaths which were the only roads.

The children learned their daily tasks from
their parents. The boys tended the herds,
and the girls shared in their mothers' work.

15

Almost everyone walked. Yet horses were not entirely unknown, as this carved figure of an African king shows. The West African kingdoms sold gold and ivory to the Arabs from the north in return for horses and other luxuries.

Later they traded with Europe, through the Portuguese who sailed down the Atlantic coast. Foreign ships also carried away captured tribesmen, to be sold as slaves. Many were taken to America.

The kings became rich and powerful.
They lived in palaces, surrounded by
courtiers and officials. Statues were
made of some kings, and cast in metal.
This was a king of Ife.

Here is a king of
Benin with his
attendants. One of
the boys supports
his arm and carries
his sword, the other
carries his cup. The
two men shade him
with shields.

17

This picture shows a chief with his attendants and emblems of rank – his pipe umbrella, sword and stick.

Almost every tribe had its chief. Although the chiefs were not as powerful as the great kings, they were respected and obeyed. Some tribes believed that the chief alone had power to bring rain.

The symbol of a chief's power might be a stool. In some tribes every man and woman had a wooden stool, which must not be used by anybody else as it was believed to contain the owner's spirit. When not in use it was laid on its side so that a strange spirit could not occupy it.

The most famous African stool is the Golden Stool of the Ashanti. Stories tell how it descended from the sky to settle on the lap of an early king when he was uniting the tribes to protect their lands against invaders. It became the symbol of the nation's well-being.

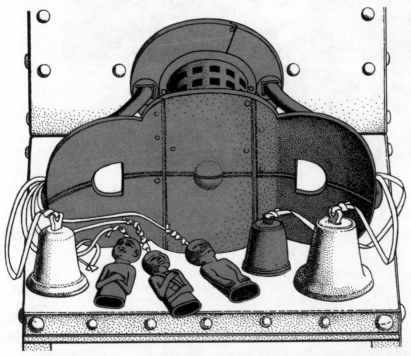

This stool of solid gold is placed like this on its side and has its own throne, as it must never touch the ground. Attached to its seat are bells, one made of gold and two of brass, and three gold figures of defeated warriors, also used as bells. In processions the stool is carried ahead of the king with the bells ringing. Being more honoured than the king himself it has its own bodyguard, shield and umbrella.

Cloths like this were made only for chiefs, or for state banners and umbrellas. The pictures were cut out of coloured material and sewn on to the cloth. Among the symbols are stools, knives, animals and birds.

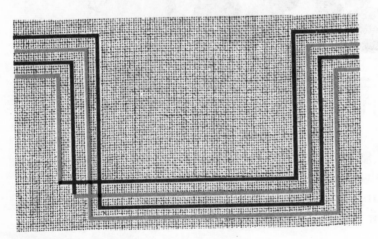

This design was called the Liar's cloth. It was worn by an Ashan chief when he heard a court case, and was believed to confuse a witness who made false statements.

20

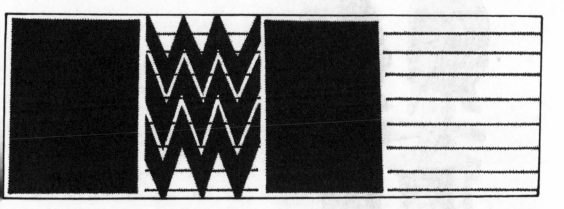

Many cloth designs had a meaning. This one showed that the wearer had recently become rich. It could only be worn by a wealthy man.

Even abstract patterns decorating a wall might have a meaning. A tribesman explains the one below like this:

The sun is in the centre, and the bands of pattern are the moon. The wavy lines are the feet of the moon. Because the moon comes and goes, it must have feet.

The local chiefs and headmen were usually the heads of important families. Family life was the centre of all activities, and when a member died he was still given offerings of food and water, and prayed to for help.

These are ancestor figures, carved in wood and believed to contain the spirits of the dead.

A chief's ancestor could become the protector of his tribe. He might even become a tribal god. The tribesmen believed in gods of many kinds, like thunder gods, an earth goddess, and a creator god.

Some tribes kept the bones of the dead. This guardian figure was attached to a basket which contained ancestral bones. It was taken off and used in religious ceremonies.

Men relied on their sons to care for them after death, so it was a great misfortune if a family was childless.

The Ashanti believed that these little dolls would enable a woman to have babies.

The tribes believed that magic could defend them against dangerous spirits, and the men who knew its secrets were powerful. For one kind of magic they carved figures like these, which we call fetishes. Some had nails driven into them, perhaps to make them more effective. Into each fetish something was put to give it power, like part of a lion for strength or of a deer for swiftness. Here a knob covers the hole in the head which holds the magic load.

24

Some figures were used for divination, to find out from the spirits why there was illness or misfortune. This figure was used by a women's society in curing the sick.

This figure of a woman with a bowl was placed outside a hut to collect gifts.
Offerings had to be made to the spirits who were asked to give help and protection.

25

Many tribes had masks, costumes or headdresses, which they used in their ceremonies. Antelope headdresses like this were worn by young men of one tribe in a fertility ceremony. Each year, before the rainy season began, they visited the fields and then returned to the town, where they danced like antelopes.

People believed that the spirits would punish them if they disobeyed tribal rules. The teenage boys were taught the rules and rituals at a special "school", which lasted several weeks. Then they were received into the men's world with ceremonies and dancing.

A number of tribes had secret societies which performed special work and knew magic that was taught only to their members. Every secret society had its own masks, carved out of wood and sometimes decorated with substances like monkey hair.

The mask above is from the Lion Society. The other was believed to protect young boys until they were admitted to the men's societies.

Most ceremonies included music and dancing. Lines of people stamped and clapped to the drum rhythms, which were often combined, like two tunes played together, giving a complicated beat.

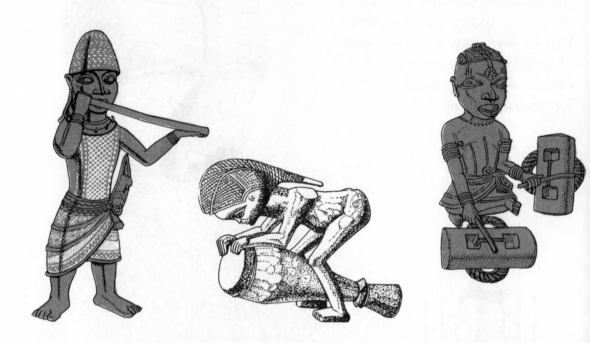

These figures are a hornblower and drummers. There were drums of ma kinds and uses. Some were used to send messages across the country. There were no roads—yet in a few hours news was known hundreds of miles away. The talking drums, as they were called, beat two different notes with which they imitated the words of ordinary speech. Distant tribes could pick up the message and beat it out again to others further away, translated if necessary into a different language.

With no written records, knowledge was passed from parents to children through stories and proverbs. This little goldweight is an animal with horns so long that they stretch beyond its back. It expresses the idea that it is useless to look back regretfully into the past.

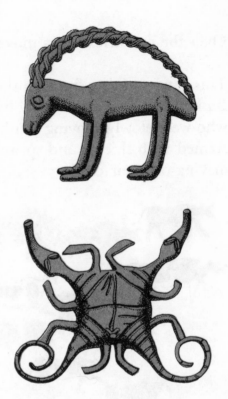

The figure of two crocodiles with a single belly was used to rebuke a selfish person, reminding him that members of a family depend on one another.

In some parts of Africa women used potlids like this to complain to their husbands. It says: "I can be open with you. Love must not only come from one side. Once I was young with a house, and everyone offered me a chair. Now I am old I get no attention."

29

Over the centuries tribes moved south through Africa, finding new land

This cave painting from southern Africa records fighting between the Bushmen, who were already living there, and the more advanced Bantu who were slowly moving south with their cattle about 500 years ago. Armed with shields and spears they attack a line of Bushmen who are driving off their cattle.

The Bushmen, who lived by hunting, stole the cattle, outraging the Bantu who prized their cows and oxen as wealth, not food. Oxen were only killed on important occasions.

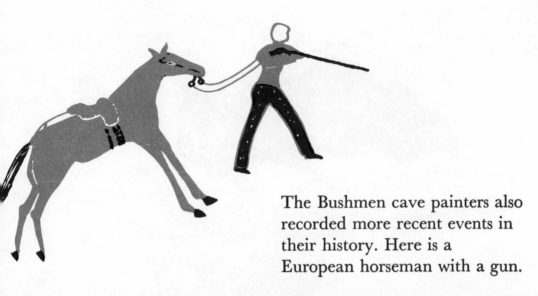

The Bushmen cave painters also recorded more recent events in their history. Here is a European horseman with a gun.

The coming of the Europeans ended the long period of isolation during which the African tribes developed their own ways of life.

A West African artist has recorded the coming of a Portuguese missionary in a ship. He is holding up a cross, the symbol of Christianity.

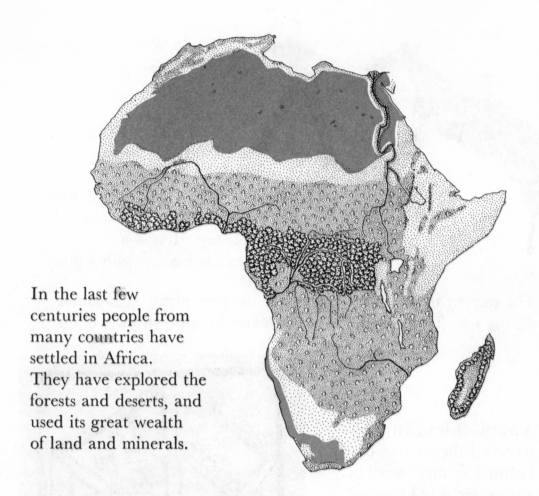

In the last few
centuries people from
many countries have
settled in Africa.
They have explored the
forests and deserts, and
used its great wealth
of land and minerals.

Tribal life is changing, and science and education are taking the
place of magic and simple farming. While new nations emerge, students
are delving into Africa's past to discover the early history of the
tribesmen whose music and sculpture have enriched and enlivened the
art of the world.

02-04-2005 12:23PM

Item(s) checked out to 2523600008243.

TITLE: Art & life in Africa [computer f

BARCODE: 1002260571ou4ug

DUE DATE: 02-25-05

TITLE: They lived like this in ancient

BARCODE: 35111000244123on1ug

DUE DATE: 02-25-05

TITLE: Ethno graphic : races, cultures,

BARCODE: 82184110114mu3ug

DUE DATE: 02-25-05

Dawes Memorial Library

740-376-4757